I AM

by

Stephanie Lauren Moore

To Sara,
Thank you for your love and support ♡
I really hope you like the book and find it comforting!
Lots of love,
Stephanie Lauren Moore
xxx

First Edition 2019.

Dedications

This book is dedicated to my mother, Angela, for always believing that I am capable of anything, and supporting me no matter what.

I'd also like to dedicate this book to my sister, Tasha, who has not only loved me unconditionally, but took me under her wing the moment I was born. Your love and support has carried me this far and will continue to motivate me for years to come.

I also dedicate this book to those family members that have continued to support me throughout all of my ventures. Dave, Joshua, Jaice, Kairi, and George.

Thank you Hannah, Jessi, Connor, and the rest of my supporting team.

Thank you to Daniel Combes for providing such an inspiring piece of photography for the cover of this book. You are incredibly talented.

I'd also like to say a huge thank you to Susan Gaigher at Influunt Publishing for turning my vision for this book into a reality. It's already a success in my eyes.

Lastly, this book is dedicated to anyone out there struggling to fight another day with mental illness. I hope you get the help you deserve. I hope this book can bring you a little joy and support.

I AM Stephanie

I personally hate it when I am reading a book and I know nothing about the author. It makes me feel like I'm unable to relate to them and their experiences. They could be offering the best advice I have ever received, but I want to get to know them as a person before I feel like I can take advice from them.

Let me introduce myself.

My name is Stephanie Lauren Moore, but I also go by about twenty-five other names. When I was 19, I was diagnosed with Dissociative Identity Disorder (DID), previously known as Multiple Personality Disorder. It's nothing scary, don't worry. To me, it just means I have a whole family inside my head that help me cope with life's anxieties. It means I'm never alone.

I like tattoos. Currently I have nine, but I would definitely like to get more. The thing with tattoos is that they are permanent and in my opinion, they should mean something special to you. Each of my body art pieces have meanings behind them. I just need to figure out what else means enough to me to have it printed onto my skin forever.

I escape my anxieties and life's problems through music. I am a firm believer that music is a language that everyone speaks. It has the power to cause you to feel intense emotions. The music and lyrics dictate how you feel, and carries incredible psychological power. Although I have never had the patience to learn an instrument, I love to sing, and I don't think I'm completely awful. My musical inspiration is John Mayer; he is incredibly talented.

Although I am only twenty years old right now, I have taken on many different jobs n my life. I've been a Quality Assurer, a Private Healthcare Specialist, an IT/Business Administrator, a Saturday Girl at a hair salon, and about ten other things. I'm now giving charity/volunteer work a go. To me, making a difference in someone's life or in the world is so much more important than punching numbers into a machine all day (no offence to anyone who actually enjoys this, of course).

I started posting videos on YouTube in 2019 to try and spread a bit of happiness, and explore ways to help people and the world in various ways. It's a slow-growing channel, but not everything happens overnight. I don't view YouTube as a career right now. I view it as a great way to spread the word about causes and events that are important to me.

What more could I ask for? Right now, my job title is just a charity/volunteer worker. I am perfectly fine with that.

"*So why don't you work in an actual job?*"

Unfortunately, due to my many health problems, both physically and mentally speaking, I am unable to commit to a 9–5 job every day of the week.

When I was just twelve years old, I had a small tumour appear in my neck. After three years of this tumour growing, pushing on my windpipe, and causing numerous other mental and physical problems, it was finally diagnosed as thyroid cancer. This year, in June 2019, I was finally given the all-clear, which was such a relief!

On top of this, I have also been diagnosed with several other health issues over the years. Just some of these are: stage-four endometriosis, IBS, hypermobility, hyper chondromalacia, tachycardia, etc. The list goes on really. The physical ailments aside, I was also diagnosed with DID, severe depression, and anxiety.

So in an ideal world, I would be at work earning money to pay the bills, and still making a difference. However, we just learn to deal with the cards we are dealt, and we make the best out of a bad situation.

I feel that all of the different challenges and trials that have been thrown my way throughout my young life so far, were what made me take an interest in charity and volunteer work. I didn't want to sit around and feel sorry for myself. I wanted to make a difference. I wanted others to feel like they could come to me for advice and support. I wanted to show others in the world that they could do anything they wanted to if they put their minds to it, no matter how awful their personal circumstances seemed.

Nowadays, although many different charities and organisations are available for mental health support and advice, I still feel that there is a lot of ignorance around the important matters. People seem to be almost afraid of talking about mental health. I want that to stop. I want mental health awareness to become the norm.

That's why I wanted to write this book. Even if only one person ever gets the opportunity to read it. Even if it only helps one person in this gigantic world. Then I have done what I was born to do. Because that's why we are all here, right? We are here to find our purpose and fulfil our destiny. I've decided that my destiny is to help others through the

experiences that I've had. I want to make people smile. Scrap that. I want to make everybody smile, at least once.
By now, it's probably obvious that I like to talk a lot and have a weird personality. Or twenty-six personalities, I should say. It's OK, I've learnt how to laugh at that diagnosis. We get along.

In this book, I'm going to share with you some of the best tips or pieces of advice I ever received. These tips helped me to where I am mentally today. I hope they will help you just as much. Throughout the book, there are activities for you to complete. This is so you don't forget where you started. I want you to see how far you will have come when you reach the end of the book.

I hope you can learn the 'I am' attitude.

> "*We may not be in control of the circumstances that present themselves in our lives, but we sure as heck control how we handle them and move forward.*"
>
> —Stephanie Lauren Moore

I AM

One of my favourite tattoos is on the back of my left foot. I got it done at the start of 2019, at Zombie Monkey Tattoos (thanks to an awesome team!). People always ask me what exactly it means. Like I said earlier, I think every tattoo should have a meaning behind it. Even if that meaning is personal and only seems to make sense to you. My tattoo simply reads 'I am'. This has a lot of meaning to me, and is exactly what I've based some of my self-help events, and this book on.

'I am' has the ability to become anything you or it want it to mean. To me, it means that I am anything I could ever imagine. I am beautiful. I am brave. I am worthy of life. I am enough. 'I am' has the power to be anything that you give it the chance to be. The question is, what will you allow it to be? What will you allow yourself to be?

'I am' is the result of positive affirmations and spending a long time practising self-love. Until you put these techniques into practice, you can't truly hold the 'I am' attitude. But don't worry, even if you haven't gotten there yet, that doesn't mean that it can't be achieved.

EVERYONE, and I literally mean EVERYONE, can learn the art of self-love and practice the 'I am' attitude. It takes time and work, but it is one of the most rewarding and beneficial things that you can do for yourself, and for your mental health. As I say in many of my videos on YouTube, I am a huge advocate for mental health and awareness around the topic. Having practiced this 'I am' attitude myself for a long time now, I can confirm that it has majorly impacted my mental health in an incredibly positive way.

I honestly believe that if a small-town girl like me, who is trying to make a difference in the world by writing this book, has gained help from these methods, it could also help so many people. If people are willing to put in the work and effort to become 'I am', the world would be a better place; full of genuinely happy people. That's what I want. I know that it's an extremely big ask, but it's a dream of mine.
What do you see when you look in the mirror? Do you see your beauty and your good traits? Do you see someone who is kind and considerate? Do you put others first? I'm not saying that to have the 'I am' attitude you need to be egotistical or see no imperfections at all. The aim is for you to see the areas in which you can improve, and strive to be the best version of yourself. You have to start loving yourself before you try to love or help others. Otherwise it just isn't going to work, and all of your efforts will fail no matter what you try. Loving yourself and telling yourself 'I am', is the start of an entire new story that you can write for yourself, your way.

Now I want you to have a really good, deep think about three things you feel that you are. They can be anything. Even if they are not necessarily positive, because do you know what? I wasn't always the most positive person. I now look back at those negative things I had to say about myself, and I realise how far I've come in respecting and loving myself. Think about it and write down three things that you are.

I AM...

I am tired

I am vunrable

I am hopeful

Congratulations! You have just taken the first step in completely changing your life and your outlook. You are on your way to becoming 'I am'.

Now answer me this, what is your 'I am' attitude going to be for you? For me, my 'I am' attitude is learning to love myself before I can learn to love others. It's becoming the best version of myself that I can be. It's putting others' needs ahead of my own, as long as it does not cause my mental or physical health to deteriorate. It is the reminder I will always give myself when I doubt my abilities. It is what I aspire to help others to become.

There are a million things 'I am' could mean for us and everyone's answers will be completely different. That's absolutely fine. We each have so many trials and influences in our life that will impact our outlook on life and perception of ourselves. Don't feel for a second that your answers have to be the same as mine or anyone else. So what is your 'I am' attitude going to be?

My I AM attitude

I am proud of you! You have taken the first steps towards becoming 'I am'.

Learning to love yourself is something that takes a long time to put into practice, and even longer to perfect. I'm not sure that anyone can truly perfect their self-love techniques to the point where they find nothing wrong within themselves. Self-love isn't about being perfect. It's about knowing you have imperfections, but deciding to love yourself despite them, while adopting a willing attitude to work on them. Self-love is acceptance; accepting yourself as you are, and loving yourself because of who you are. The Oxford Dictionary defines 'self-love' as:

"*Regard for one's own well-being and happiness.*"

This begs the question: Do you respect yourself enough to be happy? To take care of yourself? You can't truly love yourself if you don't want to look after yourself first. This means you need to look at yourself and decide what you need to do to take better care of yourself, physically and mentally. This is where self-love and self-care goes hand-in-hand.

Let's first look at taking care of your mental health, as I, personally, believe that you won't achieve physical self-love until you are in a happier space mentally.

Taking this into consideration, write down three things that you think are holding you back mentally from being the kind of person you would like to be.

In my experience, the sort of things that held me back from being able to progress mentally, were my anxieties, past regrets, present trials, and some of the people I surrounded myself with. There are, of course, a million other reasons why you could be held back from mentally feeling OK. These are for you to assess. Even if there are more than three things that come to mind, just write down the three main ones. The things that would make the biggest positive impact on your life if you could change them.

Three things holding me back

Well done! You've identified what's holding you back. That's an incredible step. I can't even explain to you how much courage that takes, and how much commitment it shows on your part for wanting to change for the better.

Look at the three areas in your life you've identified as significantly impacting your mental health in a negative way. I want you to think about them seriously.

Why do they impact your life so negatively? Why do they hold so much power over you and your emotions? After all, you are in control of your own emotions, aren't you?

Now, for each of your bullet points, ask yourself the three questions that follow.

1. Can anything be done about this situation or circumstance?

Often, we get so overwhelmed and worked up over situations that are beyond our control. This is completely natural and understandable. However, if we are unable to change something going on in our life, we need to learn to not let it consume us to the point that it puts our mental health at risk.

On the other hand, if we are able to do something about it, then why haven't we? We can spend all the time in the world moaning about a situation, and complaining that life isn't fair, but what good does that do? It may win us some sympathy, but we aren't achieving anything productive.

In order to change something, we need to make a plan and set it in motion to take back control of what's causing us so much trouble.

2. Can I change the way I look at this situation or deal with it?

Let's say we aren't able to change or do anything about the situation we are in right now. Even if we can't do anything about it right this second, what about the future? Take for example, if you are unhappy with the place you are living in right now. Perhaps, due to circumstances beyond your control, you are unable to move out right now. Perhaps you signed a lease that means legally speaking you can't leave for another couple of months. Perhaps you are unable to afford another place, or the deposit for a new home, just yet. You could be upset and complain that it's not fair and your life is being turned upside down, OR you could make the best out of a bad situation. Are you grateful for having a roof over your head in the first place? Because honestly, there are tons of people living on the street who would jump at the opportunity to take your place.

What are you grateful for? Analysing your blessings in life will always give you a fresh outlook on life.

3. What can I do, or what would it take for this to stop impacting me so much?

Going back to the previous example, you could think to yourself "This is so unfair. I just wish I had what I wanted". However, it's a lot more productive to think something along the lines of "I'll save some more money while living here, so that when I'm in my new house, I can treat myself to new furniture". You could list all the reasons to be upset, or you could plan a bright future in your new space. We are in control of how we feel about the things that happen to us. If we allow the negatives in our lives to consume us, we will be miserable. Even when it feels like we aren't in control of a situation, that lack of control is temporary. If we take a bad situation and make a plan to make it better, we are taking back control and turning our misfortunes into advantages.

Analyse the three problem areas in your life by answering the three questions discussed above.

Can anything be done about the situation?

Can I change the way I look at the situation?

What would it take for this to stop impacting me so much?

I'm not suggesting that this method is going to completely fix everything that's going on in your life. However, hopefully it gives you a more positive outlook on life, and helps you to find some comfort in coping with life's struggles.

What I would like to reiterate, though, is that all the sadness you are feeling is temporary. It can't last forever—not if you don't let it. It may seem that your entire world is falling apart today, but each day is a fresh start. Everything will work out in the end if you are willing to put in the effort to make it work.

If anything, I hope that doing this little exercise has helped you to prioritise what's important and worth worrying about in your life. Sometimes it's easy, for me especially, to prioritise my anxieties in the wrong order. I'd be worrying about something that is so much smaller than other more important things that are going on in my life. It's good to take a step back and analyse what we are stressed about, work out if it's worth the stress, and then take action to fix it. If we can't fix it, at least we can have a positive outlook. How else do you think children like me survive cancer with a smile on our faces?

In addition to thinking positively, another area that will help you mentally, is having 'me-time'. I know, what's that, right? We are all so busy nowadays with our never-ending responsibilities. We all run around like headless chickens, high on coffee and adrenaline, looking for the next road to cross before we miss the 10:30 am McDonald's breakfast cut-off.

The concept of 'me-time' crosses over into the areas of physical self-love, as well as mental health. Taking time for yourself will benefit you both mentally and physically. 'Me-time' can be whatever you want it to be.

On the next page, write down five things that you enjoy doing. These are the things that make you happy; things you can be doing when you set aside some time for yourself to relax, de-stress, and live in the moment.

Things that I enjoy doing

This is a great opportunity to take advantage of your skills to develop your talents even further. If you ever feel like you're not good at anything, you now have a list of at least five things that you could excel in. However, I don't know if attending a spa day is really a talent. Heck, if so, I would earn a medal!

The benefits of 'me-time' are endless, even if some believe it to be selfish. 'Me-time' let's you take charge of your happiness and health, which will naturally give you more energy. You will begin to de-stress and your productivity will improve. It will completely refresh your mind, enabling you to tackle the tasks ahead with a fresh outlook and positive mind-set. Plus, who doesn't love taking a little time to pamper and rewind?

Even if you think that you have an incredibly busy life and no time for yourself, I'm sure there are some small gaps in your schedule you could fit some activities into.

On a piece of paper, write down your rough weekly schedule. Look for the times that you could use to fit in some 'me-time'.

We have now looked at the ways in which we can help ourselves mentally, and how 'me-time' benefits us physically. Next I'm going to move on to the importance of grooming.

It's no secret that if we look good, we automatically feel good too. When we feel attractive, we simply radiate confidence! Let me elaborate.

Writing a book, especially one about positivity and self-love, can be quite the challenge. You won't believe me, but do you know what helps me to concentrate and feel more productive? Getting my nails, my hair, and my make-up done nicely. Honestly, feeling beautiful (or handsome) can give us a confidence boost that does wonders for productivity. If you don't believe me, try it. Before you crack on with the house chores, work or grocery shopping, get yourself ready and pampered.

Feel beautiful. I can 100% guarantee that you will be more productive when you feel better about yourself.

So do whatever it takes. Get your nails done. Get a haircut. Do your make-up. Shave your beard, or grow it out. Go shopping for new clothes. Get new glasses, or get contact lenses. Do anything that makes you feel better and more confident in yourself.

This doesn't mean that you should spend thousands on cosmetic surgery to look like the unrealistic Instagram models or celebrities that we see online nowadays. The bittersweet truth of it is that those people have spent thousands to look like that; they edit their photos and get paid to keep changing themselves to fit the 'social criteria'. They don't necessarily truly love themselves. If they did, would they really see the need to change themselves so drastically?

"The lowest lows can be magnified by 1000% just by looking at the girls on social media that I wished I could look like or be as successful as. It makes me feel like I'm failing because all of these girls the same age are rocking life and I'm just about staying afloat."

—Hannah Cullinaine

By basing our perception of beauty on models or celebrities on social media or in magazines, we are creating unrealistic standards for ourselves that we will never meet. We need to truly love ourselves for the way we are and how we look, before we decide to make alterations. If you feel like you have 100% achieved the art of self-love, and still want to alter your appearances to make you feel better, then by all means, go ahead.

The hard part comes in when we strive to be something completely different from our true selves, just to please other people. Whatever you do, or however you decide to alter your appearance, make sure you are doing it for yourself. Make yourself happy before worrying about everyone else.

How can someone else love you if you don't love yourself? You can't expect one person to love you on behalf of both of you. That's unfair, and places too much responsibility on that person. Each of you should love yourself 50%, and love each other 50%. Together, forming a whole. Team work!

"If I have money, I can give you money. If I don't have love for myself, how can I love anyone else?"

—Tasha Clark

I could give you all the quotes in the world about loving yourself and how no relationship can work without love for yourself and for your partner. But you won't believe me until you experience it for yourself.

Take me, for example. Even though I am still at the gloriously young age of just twenty years, I have had three serious relationships. The first two didn't work out, obviously. Otherwise I would be publicly proclaiming that I am cheating on three people. No. Both guys from the first two relationships were lovely, genuine, and sweet. They had work to do on themselves, but who doesn't? However, it didn't matter how kind we were, or what our intentions were. Why? Because none of us had matured enough to understand the true meaning of self-love. None of us had practised the art of loving ourselves yet. It caused arguments, insecurities and anxieties in the relationships. Last year I made a promise to myself to stay away from relationships, and take the time to work on myself. I decided to be selfish and put myself first for a change. I wanted to make myself a better person, figure out what I wanted in life and learn to love myself for who I am, before adding a relationship into the mix. I needed to learn to love myself before I could love someone else.

That's exactly what I did, and then when I least expected it, I found the person that made me feel safe and secure. He loves me as much as he loves himself. That means he treats me exactly how he would treat himself. No arguments, insecurities, or dramas. Why? Because we both have learnt to love ourselves, enabling us to give the love to each other that we deserve.

Circle your answer to the question below:

Do I love myself? **Yes** **No**

Depending on your answer, write down the ways that you have learnt to love yourself, or ways that you could learn to love yourself. These are the ways in which I want you to start practicing self-love in your daily life.

Five ways I can love myself

The more you love yourself, the more you will radiate confidence and happiness. This will attract the right kind of people into your life. Keep working on falling in love with the person staring back at you in the mirror. Still standing tall.

I AM More Than…

When I was fifteen years and forty-nine days old, the words that have the power to put the fear of death into anybody were muttered to me. These three words can change your life in an instant.

"*You have cancer.*"

The room around me started to spin. Everyone's voices became muffled; I feared that I was going deaf. Even with only fifteen years of life experience, I knew that those three words were about to cause heartache and pain. My life would change forever.

Skip forward to the following year, after all the surgeries and treatments. Lying in a hospital bed post-operation, I was told that I have stage-four endometriosis. I would never be able to carry my own children. That's quite a lot to comprehend at just sixteen years old.

Around two years later, I had two more surgeries done—one on my neck, and the other for endometriosis—and had been put into temporary medically induced menopause. This was on top of finding out that I had a hole in my heart causing irregularities and palpitations.

By this point, I think everyone would agree that I have had my fair share of health problems. Had I served my time yet? Was it over?

You bet your sweet apples it wasn't. Over the following years, IBS, chondromalacia patallae, DID, and a load of other ailments were added to my medical file. Had I won some kind of award for 'most frequent visitor to the hospital' yet? I started thinking about asking for a parking space there.

You are probably thinking, "Why on earth did I just read your entire sad life story, Steph?"

Hold your horses! Don't underestimate me just yet.

Over the past year or more I have been working very hard to maintain a positive attitude when things go to pot. I don't like people feeling sorry for me. I just want people to know my story so that it could maybe help them. After reading my life story, I'm sure you could agree that there were plenty of opportunities or reasons for me to become down or disheartened. Heck, I could have become that grumpy old lady who shouts across the yard at children to "get off my lawn" whilst constantly sporting a 'resting bitch face'. But you see, the world would be a whole better place if everyone took the things that went wrong in their life, and turned them into positives.

> "*I am more than what everybody thinks I am. I am more than just a soul trapped inside of a body that is not mine. I am more than the front that everyone else sees. I am more than what my history made me to be.*"
>
> —Hanna

For each illness or ailment that I have, I am now able to help and support others with a new diagnosis. I can use my experiences and wisdom to inform and assist them throughout their entire healing process.

This is one of the main reasons I love to do YouTube videos. For anyone out there who is struggling with something—even if I haven't been through it myself—they can see how I have turned my life around by turning my negatives into positives. If I have even helped one person in this crazy world through my writing, my acts of kindness, or my videos, then I have succeeded in fulfilling my purpose.

Apart from my various health issues, I (like so many others around the world) have faced many other different challenges and trials that have shaped me into the person that I am today. I have dealt with abuse, I've lost family and friends, left a religious background to find answers to questions I have about life, and much more. The most important thing to remember, though, is that none of these challenges define who you are as a person. People will come in and out of your life, but they will always teach you something. Their leaving doesn't reflect on you as a person. You, and you alone, decide what kind of person you want to be. There are no excuses.

Before you think I am completely heartless, I am in no way belittling you or the trials that you have been through in your life. Of course, negative challenges will heavily impact and alter our physical and mental health. Then what is it that I am trying to say?

Our mind is extremely powerful. It's the reason that things like phantom pregnancies or the physical symptoms of anxiety exist. Without even realising it, we have the power to control so much with our mind. We can't move objects and people around with our thoughts, of course. This isn't Matilda. But the mind is a powerful thing.

Read the following scenarios and think about how you would react in this situation.

1. A boy is abused mentally and physically while growing up. At the age of fourteen, he decides to run away, but

ends up living on the streets until he is nineteen years old. He begins to hang out with the wrong people, sells drugs, and gets involved with gang violence. Shortly after, his best friend is murdered. In retaliation, he murders the member of another gang who was involved. He is jailed for his actions. He blames his rough upbringing, as well as the conditions he was living in.

2. The same scenario applies. A boy is abused. He runs away. He sells drugs and becomes violent. His best friend is murdered. This triggers the young man to step back, look at his circumstances and the danger he is in. He decides to walk away from his unlawful ways. He gets himself a job, and is now helping others who have faced similar trials or are in a similar position to the one he was in. He is supporting people to get the help that he needed.

Both scenarios started out exactly the same. However, the mental attitude that the man adopted varied in each, causing very different outcomes.

Now think about yourself. Think about the trials that you have faced in your life. I don't want you to write them down, because that gives them too much power over you. We're going to focus on the positive.

On the next page, write down the good qualities or life lessons that you have obtained from facing challenges in your life, despite what may have happened to you.

There is no challenge in life that doesn't teach us a lesson in one way or another, or has the potential to make us a better person. That is a fact. Why? Because like the wonderful Kelly Clarkson sings: 'What doesn't kill you makes you stronger'.

Life lessons I learnt from my challenges

Now write down three things that you want to do or accomplish in your future as a result of growing from your trials.

Three things I want to accomplish

After all, you are more than…

I AM Grateful

Think about your life right now. How far you have come, the challenges you have faced, and the people in your life.

Write down three things you are grateful for. Just three. Any three.

Three things I'm grateful for

People nowadays don't realise that we have so much to be grateful for. It may not always seem that way, especially when we are in the middle of a tough situation, but that's the best time to look at our circumstances and take note of everything that we do have.

I received this wake-up call earlier this year, when I was fortunate enough to go on a cruise with my family. I met a wonderful woman from America who often goes to Africa to help the young school girls. Did you know that the majority of young girls and women there do not have the appropriate resources for managing their periods? Can you imagine how uncomfortable it must be to bleed for seven days or more; all over yourself, and your clothes. Add into the equation the fact that you'd have limited supplies to wash your clothes. Imagine how soul destroying that must be.

For someone who suffers from extremely bad periods from stage-four endometriosis, there have been times where I have bled non-stop for weeks on end. I have certainly taken having unlimited access to the necessary supplies and health care for granted. If this is something that you still feel you are unable to relate to, think of some of the harsh realities that we hear about nearly every single day. More and more people are becoming homeless and living on the streets. That's in all weather conditions too. There are other countries less fortunate than our own who live without sufficient food or water. Children and adults around the world are forced to stay in hospitals with heavy restrictions, due to their physical and mental ailments. Think, also, of everyone out there who would like to have their own child, but due to circumstances out of their control, they can't.

When we take a step back from the bad things that are going on in our lives, and look at the bigger picture, we realise just how much we still have to be grateful for. Did you wake up to live another day today? Be grateful that you have been given another chance to make your mark on the world, and be who you want to be.

When you really start to look outside of the box, the smaller things that we all take for granted will suddenly feel like a much bigger deal. That is when you will learn the true meaning of gratitude.

> "*Take a look at the famous painting 'The Scream' by Edvard Munch. If you are to look solely at the person in the centre screaming, you fail to see all of the beauty around them. Take a moment to appreciate the colours and the scenery in the background. Now apply that to your life and have gratitude for the beauty around you.*"
>
> —Kayleegh

Write down ten things (different from your first three) that you are grateful for in this moment. Remember to really think outside of the box.

I am grateful for...

This kind of daily exercise—reminding yourself of what to be grateful for—is a great step towards developing a more positive mind set. It will help you to see every situation in a new light, finding a positive outcome while maintaining your appreciation for what you do have.

Now I am not saying that this is an easy thing to do at all. It's certainly not a permanent fix. There are still a lot of days where I receive bad news or everything just seems to be going wrong. That's when my sister will often tell me to 'count my blessings'. It's more than alright to cry, scream and shout when something goes wrong in our lives. We are human, and that is our automatic response. However, we need to remember to pick ourselves back up and hold our heads high once again. We each have a decision to make. We can either carry on deteriorating mentally, or we can appreciate what is going right in our lives.

Always remember to start each day with a grateful heart and a smiley face.

I AM Learning

You wouldn't expect a child to understand everything about life from the moment that they are born into this world. Heck, even by the age of four or five, they still don't have a clue about what is about to hit them. We teach the children of this generation to the best of our abilities, imparting the knowledge that we have accumulated over time. We know children will make mistakes. They have to be told the same things over and over again, until they understand.

When we, as adults, are learning anything new, we are also 'beginners'. We are babies or children in the new subject we are learning. It's not expected of us to know everything right at the beginning, because we will not remember everything about the topic the first time we hear it. Just like children, we will make mistakes, forget, and sometimes just want to give up altogether. That doesn't mean that we are failing. It just means that although we are trying our very best, unfortunately sometimes our imperfections get the better of us. This is no reason to quit, though. If anything, it should give you the motivation you need to try harder than ever. After all, you are still learning.

> "*Learning means that we are growing. To stop learning would halt our growth and personal development.*"
>
> —Kensley

Everything that you will learn in this book, and many similar self-help books, will take time to practise. You will not automatically love yourself. Nor will you suddenly be the most positive person on the planet. Change takes determination, consistency, and most importantly, time. It's a process.

The word 'learning' implies action on our part. It isn't something that we can obtain passively. We need to put effort into our learning in order to progress in the way we want to. It has taken me a long time to get to the place where I am now mentally. That being said, I still have a long way to go. Making a big and life-altering change doesn't happen overnight. However, you will definitely see positive changes within yourself from very early on in your personal development process. It's good to write down and keep track of these positive improvements when you notice them.

I have been learning to...

The good thing about learning taking time is that you don't have to rush your development process. You can pick specific areas that you'd like to focus on first, rather than overwhelming yourself trying to change too much, too quickly. In this regard, it's very important to take a close look at yourself and honestly determine what to prioritise in your learning first.

Write down, in order of priority, what you'd like to work on about yourself. Next to each one, detail a few simple ways that you can do this.

I want to work on...	I will do this by...

The best thing is that there is no deadline or time limit for any of this. You are the one who is learning, and therefore, you can take it at your own pace.

> "*Learning is a journey, not a race. There is no first place so enjoy the ride. Do it for yourself rather than anyone else.*"
>
> —Scarlett

Keep going! You are doing great!

I AM Finding My Purpose!

When I was four years old, I found my voice, and I was always singing. I was determined that I would be the next Whitney Houston. I had karaoke machines, microphones, and a variety of instruments. You would never hear me not singing. It drove my family insane!

Then, when I was around seven years old, I wanted to become a teacher. I would make pretend lesson plans, registers, and school books. I even had a whiteboard and pen that I used to teach invisible classrooms in my bedroom.

At the age of eleven, I made the final decision that I wanted to be a crime scene investigator. More specifically, a forensic scientist. I would collect "evidence" (usually loose items from around the house), "bag them" in sandwich bags, and "test them" with various soaps and perfumes that I could find. I was goofy, and quite the nerd.

As you know, I did not pursue any of those careers I aspired to when I was little. But, like any child, I was determined to find the answer to the question that every young person is asked:

"*What do you want to be when you grow up*?"

How on earth, as kids, are we supposed to know the answer to such a complex question? When we are young, we don't have the life experience to comprehend what we should dedicate our lives to. We could barely choose what colour to paint our clay rockets, let alone what career we should pursue. However, notice that the question doesn't automatically imply that we should chase some sort of dream job. It's asking who and what type of person do we want to be? And when we are young and innocent, we have the ability to become anything we want to.

Rather than pondering what sort of career we want in life, we should be taught how to figure out what our purpose is.

Our purpose can cover a multitude of jobs. For example: If your purpose is to teach, you could work in a school, teach languages abroad, become a life coach, etc. If your purpose is to help people, you could become a nurse or doctor, work in a charity or volunteer setting, become a therapist, coach in rehabilitation centres, etc. If your purpose is to seek justice, you could become a lawyer or judge, work for the police department, be a crime scene investigator, etc. I'm sure you get the point.

By figuring out your purpose in life, you are creating more opportunities for yourself. But how on earth do you find your purpose? It's different for everyone, so there is no fixed system to figuring it out.

The activities that follow are a good starting point to help you find your purpose. Write down:

Three hobbies I enjoy

Three things I'd like to learn more about

Three topics I am passionate about

Five skills I have

On the next page, write down how your skills are useful in any of the above areas:

How my skills are useful

Which area or topic stood out the most to you when answering these questions? While writing your answers, did you notice that you were completely focused on you, your happiness and your good qualities? Maybe this is the first time you have been concerned about yourself in a long time.

Now think about all your answers, as well as the questions, and decide what sort of purpose they fit. Only you can decide. Once you have figure this out, you will have unlocked a world of opportunities for yourself. It doesn't matter what age you are either. You are never too young nor too old to start learning or taking control of your life.

Top three areas I want to learn more about

Hopefully, by now you feel a bit supported in your journey to finding your purpose. If not, keep pondering the questions that you answered on the previous page, and decide when the right time would be to pursue these new dreams. Sometimes our circumstances, through no fault of our own, won't allow for us to pursue our purpose. Don't let this dishearten you. Just allow yourself the time to grow stronger, and wait for the appropriate time.

What is important to remember is, just like our dream jobs when we were children, our purpose in life can change and adapt as we grow. Initially we may want to teach to fulfil our purpose. However, after maybe ten years or so, we may eventually decide to pursue something else. This does not mean that we have wasted our time on a purpose not meant for us. It means that as we develop personally, the circumstances around us may change and impact our life in a way that suggests we pursue something else. Something better! If this happens to us, it is completely normal, and we should not fight it. It just means that our skills are needed elsewhere. And who doesn't want to feel needed?

Write down three things you can focus on to find and achieve your life's purpose.

Three things I can focus on to achieve my purpose

"*Finding your life's purpose is like looking for a holiday. You search based on your wants, needs and preference. You select the one that will make you happiest. Apply this when hunting for your purpose and you're good to go.*"

—Lana

I AM Who I Am

In the first part of this book, I told you a little bit about myself. I wish I was able to ask you a little bit about yourself and get to know you. You were interested in reading my book, for a start. That makes me extremely happy and grateful. So, thank you. It also tells me that you are looking to improve yourself for the better. That too is so commendable.

This book is designed to get you thinking about everything you can work on, and all of the things that you could be. But it's just as important to also consider who you already are. You are incredible and worthy. You don't give yourself enough credit for what an amazing human you are. You are worthy of self-love, and deserve appreciation.

Write down five things that make you unique.

Five things that make me unique

The things that others may think are weird about you, are really your best features! There is no one on this earth who is like you. When you really take the time to comprehend that, it is mind blowing. There are eight billion people on this planet, and no one is anything like you. You are a treasure. You are you.

It's time to say "screw you" to the worlds' view of what perfection looks like, and hold your head high. It's time to appreciate everything that you are. No matter where you come from, the challenges you have faced, or the things you wish you could have changed, you are here. There is certainly no reason to ever apologise for being who you are.

There may be many people from older generations or religions that don't agree with your lifestyle choices, but it is your life, and not theirs. No other human on this earth has the right to tell you how to live your life (unless you are doing illegal or dangerous things). As long as you aren't harming anyone else, then what you do is no one else's business. You deserve to be happy just as much as anyone else.

I have many friends who are in the process of transitioning to become their true preferred gender. I have friends who are covered in tattoos and piercings. I have friends who, like myself, swear on a daily basis in a non-aggressive way. I have a selection of colourful wigs that I wear whenever I feel like it. I have friends who all have different sexual preferences. I have friends who have different styles and fashion choices. I have absolutely nothing against religions or peoples' beliefs. But I do believe that we are supposed to live a life that makes us feel happy.

I have tattoos, but that doesn't make me any less of a woman, or mean that I'm unkind in any way. I have DID, but that doesn't make me crazy. I am many things to many different people, but that doesn't matter, because I am who I am.

Think about everything about yourself that makes you happy. It can be physical, mental, or spiritual. It can be a quality or a skill, an appearance trait or a habit.

Write down the things that make you happy and explain why they make you happy.

What makes me happy and why?

Never allow anyone to take these things away from you or make you feel guilty about them. If they do, they are slowly taking away your happiness. Enjoy and appreciate that you have these things that bring you joy. Keep doing the things that make you happy, because they are what make you feel like yourself. These are just some of the things that make you, you.

I'm a big advocate for no judgement. I believe everyone is entitled to their own opinion, as long as any negative comments are not voiced publicly. I also believe you shouldn't have to follow a certain lifestyle to be accepted, especially if it is mentally damaging or detrimental to your health. However, everyone is entitled to their personal opinion, and this is just my own.

You are the only person who matters when it comes down to your happiness. You make all the calls in your life. Although people can give you their suggestions, your opinion is the only one that matters at the end of the day.

A few weeks ago a woman posted something about her new nose piercing in one of my support groups. She had wanted one for years. She was in her late twenties, a mum of two, and had finally built up the courage to take the plunge and get the piercing. She was so excited, and posted a beautiful photograph of it on her social media. However, the comments she received weren't complimentary or positive. She was faced with rejection from family and friends who asked her if "it was a joke", and told her to take it out. This, in my opinion, is far from alright. Nobody, and I mean NOBODY, should ever be made to feel guilty or ugly for a decision they made about their appearance. Especially not supposed family and friends. She was so excited to get this piercing, and it took a lot of courage. To be knocked down like that, to the point of questioning her decision, is disgusting. Girl, if you are reading this, then please know that you looked beautiful. Own it and work it.

No matter what decisions you make for your own well-being and happiness, own it. It's no one else's responsibility to make you happy. Unfortunately that task is left to each of us to achieve on our own. No one can question why you have made the decisions that you did, because they are not in your position. They are not you.

You are never going to be for everyone. There will be people who just don't 'click' with you. There will be others that will be jealous of you, or won't like you for reasons you will never understand. Others will never even try to make an effort with you, but will state that they do not like you. This is alright.

It's impossible to make everyone happy, and you will never be able to have everyone like you, no matter how nice you are. It's not your fault, so you should never ever change or alter yourself for anyone else. Even if that's what seems like the right thing to do at the time. People will also change around you, but you have to stay true to your authentic self. Never allow anyone to control who you are just so you can gain their approval. Be you.

Today is the day that you need to take control of your happiness and accept exactly who you are. There is so much about you that is worth appreciating and even celebrating.

Write down who you are.

I am...

It's time to learn to love and accept yourself. Love and accept all the good and the bad. The mistakes, the decisions, the imperfections, and the good qualities. Celebrate yourself for who you are.

You are who you are.

I AM Fearless

Everyone is born with fears. Even as a newborn, a baby is afraid of its mother leaving. It will cry if it feels alone. As the baby grows into a child, the usual fears will emerge; monsters, the dark, spiders. As we grow up, it's almost looked down upon to have fears, because we are adults. But everyone has fears. Whether it's a fear of death, an animal, a feeling, or yoghurt lids (it's certainly not me that has an irrational fear of yoghurt lids…). These days, many adults will convince themselves that they do not have any fears. But upon talking deeper with them, you will find that they hold onto many fears, often ones that most of us feel too. However, we can still act fearless despite our everyday fears.

Write down three things that you are afraid of.

Three things I'm afraid of

It actually isn't really our fears that make us fearful. It's our attitude towards them. If we are so scared of something that it prevents us from being able to live our life properly, or engage in activities that we would like to, that's when we become fearful. Our actions regarding our fears are what determine whether we will be fearful or fearless.

Let me elaborate. A woman is insecure about her body after she has given birth to three children over the years. She refuses to go to any swimming pool or beach where a bathing suit is required. This is a fearful attitude, because the fear itself is preventing her from doing the activities she'd enjoy in life. After spending time working on her self-love and body positivity, she makes the decision to take her children to the beach. She wears a modest swimming costume and enjoys playing in the sea with her children. She feels content, making new memories with her family, and feels more confident. This is a fearless attitude. Rather than avoiding the fear itself, she tackles it head-on, and is rewarded with a positive outcome.

"*Life shrinks or expands in proportion to one's courage.*"
—Anais Nin

Write down some things you could do to overcome your fears.

Things I can do to overcome my fears

The hard truth that we need to learn in life, is that tomorrow is never guaranteed for any of us. Once we fully comprehend that fact and accept it, our whole perception of life will change. We will start to live for ourselves rather than anyone else. We will let go of all of our fears and start ticking things off our bucket lists. We may even get to add new things to our bucket lists that we didn't have the confidence to add before. We need to forget the past, forgive our own and others' mistakes, love ourselves, and put our happiness first.

By becoming fearless, you are basically saying "I am in control of my feelings and my destiny". I am convinced that all of us have at least one thing in common—we want to feel in control of our lives.

Trying to change or adapt for the better definitely takes guts, and requires a fearless attitude. Why? Becoming fearless requires an open mental attitude and needs willingness on your part. You will be rediscovering yourself in a whole new light, and opening your eyes to things that you didn't see before. You may need to change certain thinking patterns to learn to love yourself. You may even dislike the process, or dislike some of the constructive criticism you receive. However, the art of being fearless will help you to remain focused on your end goal, while learning and developing in the best possible way.

A lot of the time, it's actually our insecurities that hold us back from doing things, rather than the fear itself. We are scared that we won't be good enough, or that we lack the right skills. We're afraid of how it will look; we may think it looks crazy from the outside. I'm here to tell you to let those insecurities go. Anything is possible. I recently heard about a ninety-four-year-old woman who attended Southern New Hampshire College. She received her bachelor's degree with a 4.0 GPA in 2017. It is never too late to go after what you want in life.

You are capable. You may look crazy—heck you may even be crazy for what you want to achieve—but how did it look when Wilbur and Orville Wright told the world they would create flying machines that would take people from one place on the earth to another? You have the ability to create something incredible. You have the skills to make a change so big in the world that you can't even comprehend it right now. When you start to believe in yourself and realise how talented and incredible you are, you will become capable of so much more.

Whatever it is you would like to achieve or do in life, just take the leap. Be fearless.

Write down what you want to achieve or do in life.

I will...

I AM Not Sorry

"*I'm sorry.*" I grew up with abuse from a narcissist. Unfortunately, my sister also suffered the same emotional and mental abuse. The effect this had on us was that we were always ready to apologise, even for things that didn't involve us in the slightest.

You spilt your tea? I'm sorry. You hurt your back? I'm sorry. You don't like my personality? I'm sorry. For the majority of our lives, we felt guilty if we did not apologise for anything and everything. I honestly feel like there must be thousands around the world who do the exact same thing, perhaps without even realising it. Of course, not everyone will have fought through some form of abuse.

We were all raised in a society where we're expected to apologise for ourselves and our imperfections. We are taught that we need to apologise for not looking, acting or existing in a certain way. Why?

I say "NO MORE!". I'm telling you now to say "Screw it, I am NOT sorry!"

We need to learn to erase the negative thinking of apologising for who we are. We are exactly who we are meant to be, and we have nothing to be sorry for. I have tattoos, I have stretch marks, I curse, I buy too many clothes, I have a crazy personality, I have scars, and I am certainly not sorry for any of it. It's me.

On the next page, write down a list of everything that makes you, you.

What makes me ME

Now write down: "I am not sorry for any of it".

The most famous and beautiful model of her time was Miss Marilyn Monroe. She was not a size four, she had curves, and she also suffered from endometriosis. Did any of those things make her less beautiful or worthy of the fame she acquired? Not at all. She was insanely beautiful inside and out, and people admired the confidence she radiated. Instead of apologising for not looking the way everyone expected her to look like as a model, she embraced her appearance and made her imperfections beautiful to the world. She was one of the first few women who broke the status quo and made their own rules.

If we were all too focused on how everyone else viewed us, we would have no time for ourselves. We wouldn't practice self-love, enjoy 'me-time', or develop in the way that we want to. What is the point of spending all that time trying to be someone that you aren't, to please people that will never truly accept you for yourself. You deserve to walk out into the world the way that you choose to, and you deserve to do it confident that you are not sorry for the way you are. You need to march out into the world and say "Take me as I am, or not at all". As soon as you stop living life for yourself, and apologise for not being the person everyone expects you to be, you lose respect for yourself.

Never ever be sorry for living life the way you want, searching to find what you are looking for, or wanting what you rightfully deserve. Never apologise for having to walk away from people or situations that get in the way of you developing and accomplishing your goals. Your goals, decisions, personality or attitude shouldn't impact another human's life in such a way that you should feel the need to apologise. You should be striving for happiness. The people who truly care about you and love you, will support you and your decisions. If it affects their life in a negative way, it is a problem that lies within them. Not you.

There is never going to be a situation where you should feel the need to justify yourself in some way. This is YOUR life. You should never be put in a spot where you need to explain yourself or the decisions you have made. If anyone ever makes you feel like that, get rid of them. That type of unnecessary negativity will interrupt any self-love progression or personal development.

On the next page, write down the reasons why you should never apologise for who you are. Whenever you feel the need to justify who you are or apologise for being you, remind yourself of these qualities and reasons you gave yourself why you shouldn't be ashamed. Do not apologise for being you!

Why I should not apologise

You are pretty cool.

I AM ENOUGH

We are almost at the end of this journey. Look how far you have already come. Hopefully by now you have started to apply some of the lessons you've learnt in this book in your life. Maybe when looking back at your answers to the earlier questions, you will notice how much you have personally developed already. Would you answer the questions differently now? If not, there's no need to worry. These changes and your progression will come over time. You just need to keep coming back to these lessons and practice them daily.

Something that took me a very long time to understand and believe, was to learn my worth and trust that I am enough. This isn't easy, but you can do it too. You will need to embody everything that you have learnt in this book, and apply it to your life. You have to work hard and begin to fall in love with the person staring back at you in the mirror. Every lesson that I have incorporated into this book will help you to see your worth, as long as you heed its advice.

So why is it so important for us to feel like we are enough?

First of all, when we feel worthy and good enough, hormones such as dopamine and serotonin are released. These are also known or referred to as the 'happy hormones'. You're essentially filling up your body with positive energy and emotions.

Second, based on the 'Law of Attraction', whatever you think about, comes about. If this is true, the more confidence that you demonstrate, and the more positivity that you extend to others, the more confidence and positivity will come back to you in various ways.

Once you begin to feel good enough, you will make more well-informed decisions, feel better mentally and physically, and acquire many attractive qualities. Feeling this way becomes a sort-of 'healthy addiction'. When you start to feel good and see the positive changes within yourself, you will become motivated to carry on and push yourself even further.

More often than not, we are the ones who think that we are not good enough. You are your own worst enemy, holding a knife to your throat. It's up to you to take away that metaphorical knife, and free up your mind to work on yourself in a positive way.

If you spend too much of your time and focus on not feeling good enough, you never will be. If you believe that you are not good enough, you will base your life and decisions according to your 'limitations'. You won't step out of your comfort zone or pursue new goals. For example, I could have easily felt inadequate to write this book. However, I saw a need, and I wanted to help others. I believed that I was enough.

Never feeling 'good enough' also takes away whatever control we do have in our life. It's us giving into that feeling that we can't do anything, therefore we won't even try. Humans have the ability to learn and perfect anything we want to. To start the process, we just have to have a willing attitude and believe that we are enough.

On the next page, write down ten things that make you feel that you ARE good enough.

I am good enough

Now write down five things that you CAN do that you haven't yet done due to feelings of inadequacy.

Five things I can do

Whenever you start to feel like you are not good enough, remind yourself of the traits that you have listed on the previous page. Remember that you are capable of anything. Go and pursue the above list, make new memories, and show the world who you are.

You Are Enough!

You ARE

Well done! You have reached the end of this book. By reading and participating in the activities presented here, you have demonstrated a clear desire to improve yourself and your mental well-being. Hopefully the different techniques in this book will help you along your personal development journey.

I encourage you to look back now and then at the questions and answers you gave here, to see how you progress over time. You'll be surprised at how much you have progressed without even realising it, just by following some simple tips in this book.

It's now time to put everything that you have learnt into practice. Start to believe that you are whatever you want to be. You are worthy, and you are enough.

Remember to always take your time, put your mental health first, and acknowledge your achievements as you grow. Never disregard any of the progress you make, no matter how big or small it is. Keep referring back to this book for reminders and refreshers whenever you need to.

Don't give up.

So, do you have the 'I AM' attitude?

47273142R00038

Printed in Poland
by Amazon Fulfillment
Poland Sp. z o.o., Wrocław